This I Know

Resting in Grace

J. Lauraine Johnson

This I Know – Resting in Grace

Copyright © J. Lauraine Johnson, 2023

All rights reserved. No part of this book may be reproduced or used in any form without permission from the author, except for brief quotations in critical reviews or articles.

Scripture quotations marked (NIV) are taken from the Holy Bible, New International Version®, NIV®.
Copyright © 1973, 1978, 1984 by Biblica, Inc.™
Used by permission of Zondervan. All rights reserved worldwide.

Scripture quotations marked (NLT) are taken from the Holy Bible, New Living Translation, copyright © 1996, 2004, 2007 by Tyndale House Foundation. Used by permission of Tyndale House Publishers, Inc., Carol Stream, Illinois 60188. All rights reserved.

Scripture quotations marked "MSG" or "The Message" are taken from The Message. Copyright 1993, 1994, 1995, 1996, 2000, 2001, 2002. Used by permission of NavPress Publishing Group.

Scripture quotations taken from the (NASB®) New American Standard Bible®, Copyright © 1960, 1971, 1977, 1995, 2020 by The Lockman Foundation. Used by permission. All rights reserved. lockman.org

jlaurainejohnson@gmail.com

ISBN 978-1-7388354-0-9

Dedication

To my husband, Gord, for his unfailing support and love.

To my daughters, Lauren, my first gift, and Alise, my second gift.

Cover art dedicated in loving memory of my son-in-law Brett (1987-2022).

Table of Contents

Introduction 11
Chapter 1 – Rear View 17
- Faultlines 17
- Reconstruction 19
- Burdened 24

Chapter 2 – Chrysalis 29
- Faith and Works 29
- Two Kinds of Faith 37
- Abiding 40

Chapter 3 – Emergence 45
- Into the Light 45
- Freedom 49
- Rest 53

Chapter 4 – Final Word 57
- Love 57

Postscript 61
Appendix 65
- Abraham 66
- Achievement and Self-Worth 69
- Christ, My Righteousness 72

- Conviction and Condemnation 76
- Romans 8:28 80
- Wisdom 84

Thought Anchors 91

Scripture References 93

Acknowledgements

Thank you to Nancy, Miriam and Dennis, Margaret, and Gail for what you provided during a particularly difficult time in my life. You gifted me beyond measure. Thank you to Gayle for faithfully standing beside me as both sister and friend.

Thank you to Alice for reading the first draft of the manuscript and offering your encouragement and suggestions.

Gord, you know what I am trying to say. Thank you for pressing me toward clarification.

Thank you to Janaya for suggesting that I write an introduction to this manuscript.

Thank you to Tim for reading the final draft of the manuscript and offering greatly appreciated feedback. The 1983 vignettes provided valuable background. I am grateful for the idea.

Thank you to Ann and her team for bringing this manuscript to completion for publication.

1983

The door to the small room in Emergency is shut. This will be the last of a succession of interviews.

Tell me how you feel.

I feel like an empty carcass with no soul.

* * * * *

I face my pastor. Say something. Help me. Please.

I am afraid all the time. It won't stop. I always have a sensation of terror. Especially at night.

"*The Bible says, 'Perfect love casts out fear.' Maybe you aren't loving Gord (husband) or Lauren (daughter) enough. Maybe you should just try loving more.*"

* * * * *

My doctor stands beside my hospital bed. I confess. I didn't feel comfortable with Dr. (psychiatrist) when we were talking. I don't know where he's coming from.

The only thing you need to know is that he's coming from [Zero Street] first thing in the morning.

* * * * *

The nurse regards me with a pitying sort of look. I feel small.

I used to run a whole classroom and now look at me.

* * * * *

The steps are rock-hard. The darkness engulfing.

I need to get used to what hell will be like.

* * * * *

My words are coming out garbled. I can't say anything intelligible. Does my tongue work? What's wrong with me?

We need to give her something to counter the effects of that drug.

* * * * *

The crib is leaving the house. I can't even care for my own child. I am nothing.

* * * * *

God is gone. He has abandoned me. I can't get him back. Where are you when I need you most?

WHAT DO YOU WANT FROM ME?!

* * * * *

I. Am. So. Alone. Forever.

Introduction

The extent to which I act from fear is the extent to which I cannot act from love. This is what I most wish to communicate in this book.

What you are about to read is an edited collection of reflections and insights I wrote between 1984 and 1985. Some sentences have been lifted directly from the text of my original journal. My twenty-nine-year-old self who picked up a pen was in the process of a massive transformation, which has immeasurably blessed me ever since.

The watershed year of my life is 1983.

It started with what felt like an electric shock coursing through my body, startling me out of my sleep in the early hours of a spring morning. And so began chronic insomnia, the hospitalizations (the final of three lasting almost a month), the variety of drugs, the suicidal impulses, the terror, and the hopelessness. But it had really begun long before then. That night was only the culmination of many months.

As you read these pages, you will meet me before the date I started writing my journal. Sometimes I am writing from the vantage point of the present as I look back on my former self. I will describe the thinking that shaped me long ago, its impact, and its consequences. I will share how that thinking changed, and you will meet the person who emerged as a result.

The person before 1983 was one whose identity was wrapped up in her profession and accomplishments. I had no idea how to live in the present and *truly* relax into life. An uncomfortable ripple of unease was always lurking in the background. Living under the constant weight of "I should" and the need for measurable achievement were the hallmarks of my life. I constantly worried that I wasn't meeting what I perceived to be the expectations of others or God. None of my friends would have ever been able to detect my internal turmoil, and I made a habit of distracting myself from the nagging discomfort through perpetual busyness.

The person following 1983 was on the road to gradual healing from a slow slide into depression, which ultimately led to acute illness and subsequent hospitalizations. This occurred after my first child turned a year old. Although I sought it several times, I was not provided with the appropriate treatment to rescue me from accelerating decline.

It is important to tell you that I did not feel God at all during that tortuous period. I felt utterly abandoned. But he was there. Like Jacob, I can *now* confidently say, "Surely the Lord is [was] in this place, and I wasn't even aware of it!" (Genesis 28:16).

The medical attention I finally received enabled me to get well. But the ravages of depression had exacted a heavy toll. I just couldn't try anymore. I was mentally incapable of thinking beyond the present moment. I could not permit myself to worry about anything. Physically, I was unable to maintain any continuous activity beyond ten minutes without tiring. So I spent a lot of time sitting with my young daughter as she and I played, and going on meandering walks together. I could not tolerate the thought of deadlines or obligations. This was immensely beneficial, as it was through slowing down and resting my mind that I became capable of receiving and practising what I will be sharing.

I want to be clear that I absolutely do not believe God allowed the illness I suffered to achieve a higher purpose. That is not the meaning of "In all things God works for the good of those who love him, who have been called according to his purpose" (Romans 8:28).[1] I believe with all my heart that God is redemptive. He can take the unwelcome events of our lives and create something from the ashes. I believe in beginnings and resurrection. That is the hope from which I live. The pages I wrote so long ago, resulting in this book, are the fruit of my redemption.

Ingrained mental habits take a long time to break free of. Even though I had a new template for living, for several years, I often felt as if I were being derailed as

---

[1] See Appendix: Romans 8:28

I began the bumpy transition from one track of thinking to another. I posted pertinent scripture verses and other important thought anchors on the door of my bedroom that kept me grounded as I moved forward in my chosen direction. My new ways of thinking were reflected in fresh priorities as I learned how to live in the grace of God and shed the destructive achievement/self-worth/value paradigm that had held me in its grip.

The loose sheets of my random journaling have been sitting in a black folder, untouched for decades. In preparing to write this book, I read through the entire journal for the first time. I noted (and relived) the amazement and joy I experienced at the time of its original writing. The insights that flowed from my pen altered the trajectory of my life irrevocably. I had thought that someday I might make them shareable. That time is now.

Chapter 1

Rear View

Faultlines

Are you tired? Worn out? Burned out on religion? Come to me. Get away with me and you'll recover your life. I'll show you how to take a real rest. Walk with me and work with me—watch how I do it. Learn the unforced rhythms of grace. I won't lay anything heavy or ill-fitting on you. Keep company with me and you'll learn to live freely and lightly. (Matthew 11:28-30)

It's amazing how much energy is expended through worry and anxiety. You just don't realize it until you no longer have the capacity to engage in either. Underlying sources of anxiety are particularly difficult because you don't know where they are coming from;

you don't know how to address them, precisely because they are unknown. You are not aware of how pervasively they affect you, and how they influence what you think and do. They are subterranean, the basement, the foundation upon which you build the house that is called your life. The foundation forms the basis of what you believe, and most importantly, *why*. It informs and directs your activities and the reasons for them, interactions and the nature of them, and why you can or can't have peace in the deepest part of your being.

The foundation is unseen, but it affects everything. And eventually, any cracks or distortions in a foundation will affect what sits on top of it. The whole thing has to come down, the foundation smashed, re-poured, and the house rebuilt. The new structure will be different, built on a brand new stable foundation.

In my case, flawed foundational beliefs provoked false guilt and anxiety; they generated a "doing" sort of life as opposed to a "being" sort of life. They did not provide peace. The Bible says you are what you think (Proverbs 23:7). If the thinking changes—and most critically, a solid rationale for that change—you will be a different person.

It was a stunning discovery to realize that what I *thought* was the truth—the "truth/thinking" on which my actions were predicated—was, in fact, constricting, soul-destroying, and the very opposite of life-giving. I was under a tremendous burden that made me weary.

I discovered the truth to be incredibly liberating. My distorted thinking could not possibly have produced "peace and joy in the Holy Spirit" (Romans 14:17).

Reconstruction

Being sick flattened me. I had to rebuild my life from the bottom up. The foundational beliefs upon which I structured my life were smashed. At my core, I hadn't consciously abandoned the bedrock of the Christian faith; it's just that I didn't have the energy or desire to think about any of my previous convictions anymore. Going forward, my thinking was completely rebuilt brick by brick, resulting in a very different way of approaching life. This mental restructuring fundamentally changed the "why" of what I did; it thoroughly confronted the reason I was so driven, and gave me a solid reason to go forward on a new path of living in grace. The unfolding of what I will be sharing in this book rests on the following foundational truths I have discovered:

1. God is committed to me.
2. God doesn't want my *effort*. He wants my *heart* first and foremost.
3. Works are the inevitable consequence of abiding in Christ.

These profound, life-altering realizations cannot be overstated. They did not come about from my capacity to reason; overthinking has always been a tendency of mine. The fact is, a metaphorical curtain was gradually pulled back, and I saw. Most importantly, I saw when I wasn't expecting anything. God showed up at a time when I had no energy or ability to try to figure out a single thing. He took the initiative. And during those many months when I could no longer exert myself, God was able to dislodge deep-rooted, powerful misconceptions which both informed and motivated how I lived. Thankfully, I came to understand that

God is committed to me whether or not I "feel" it. This was the first brick of my rebuilt life.

I didn't know this. Somehow, I thought I had to do all the work. I continually analyzed my actions and the motivation behind each of them. I frequently rooted around to see if there was any sin that needed confessing. I thought all this thinking would result in spiritual maturity. I anxiously pressured myself to look for opportunities to share my faith. I was constantly afraid I might not be fulfilling what I thought I was supposed to be doing as a Christian, and was always worried about not having done enough. This is because I lived with the belief that if I were serious about my faith, I needed to try hard; I thought it was required of me. It was the trying that demonstrated my heart's orientation toward God, or so I thought.

I was in a trap of thinking I had to *do* things to prove the authenticity of my commitment. So I not only became used to but expected to live with the disquiet that came from trying and not knowing if my effort was acceptable or adequate. But there can be no peace in that. I was in a constant state of feeling unsatisfied and restless, perpetually burdened with nagging anxiety. My own voice drowned out what God would say to me about its source and how I could be free.

Amazingly, I had put *myself* in charge. My unconscious foundational belief was that if I stopped worrying about my spiritual growth, I wouldn't grow. And if I stopped fretting and thinking about it all the time, God would think I didn't care and would be displeased with me. For that reason, I was unable to abandon worrying. I simply couldn't take the risk.

But what I believed just wasn't true. It was absolutely false. Over time, my eyes were opened to what is *actually* God's truth, rather than my distortions of Scripture upon which my faulty thinking was based.

The truth affected me profoundly. It enabled me to grasp the implications of God's love in a way that had so far eluded me. I did not realize how much God is *for* me (Romans 8:31). This means that:

- **God will speak to me.** *Therefore,* I can trust that God will communicate when and how he chooses to do this. The Spirit of God does the revealing. I just need to be receptive.

- **God will guide me.** *Therefore*, I can rest. I don't have to be fearful about whether or not I'm on the "right" or "wrong" path. He will redirect me as needed, in response to my openness.

- **God will convict me.** *Therefore*, I don't need to probe for un-confessed sin. I just need to be open to God's voice and trust that he will show me what is required for my good.

- **God will guide me in pointing people toward Christ.** *Therefore*, I don't have to keep an inventory of my service or "impact." In fact, neither is important to be aware of. Because of God's commitment to me, I no longer feel compelled to focus on myself out of fear. Self-reflection is healthy, life-giving, and important to moving forward in growth; it is entirely different from the fear-driven self-evaluation in which I was engaged.

Burdened

The fundamental word foreign to how I lived my life was "rest." I always felt rest*less* but could never identify why.

My life was largely driven by a goal to measure up with my doing and trying, but I never quite knew what the goal was. Does God have a sliding scale on which he judges the significance or amount of service I perform? Has he determined a point at which he is pleased with the degree of my busyness? Does God require that I knock myself out with exhaustion to meet his approval? Is he disappointed if I don't accomplish enough? What is enough? How could I know?

Jesus invited the weary and burdened to rest, but I didn't have the slightest idea what that meant. I had no insight whatsoever as to why I couldn't just stop and pull back---mentally and physically. Life felt like a perpetual assault of obligations and expectations. But they were self-imposed. And now that I had no choice but to cease striving while recuperating from my illness, I came to realize what rest actually felt like and how my life could be lived differently. Since I simply couldn't try to *achieve* any longer, I learned how to completely disconnect how I felt about myself according to my accomplishments and successes or lack thereof. This novelty was both wonderfully releasing and completely unfamiliar.

Fear drove me into trying hard. I feared the disapproval of others. I feared God's disapproval. I subconsciously feared I might be rejected in the end for not doing enough. I lived contrary to my own belief that I was saved by grace and not by the things I did. However, being motivated by fear and resting in grace cannot co-exist. They are mutually exclusive. Fear is a thief. It robbed me of both peace and rest. It prevented me from fully engaging with the present moment and the people in front of me. Because worry is such an insidious distraction, my mind was always partly somewhere else.

I lived in a paralyzing stranglehold of "as a Christian I should." "I haven't done enough" was a recording that played out in my head all the time (e.g. phone this person, read my Bible). I felt God was my slave driver, although I could never have admitted this. I believed intellectually that God loved me, but I did not realize he was an ally in my journey—that he was on my side. The truth is, I was afraid of him, and I didn't know how to resolve this tension of affirming grace while believing God was making relentless demands on me, which, if I were honest, I resented.

I felt the unwanted pressure of performance, but I didn't know the way out from under it. I wanted freedom. Deep inside, I silently cried out, "When can I stop trying? I want to stop. I want to be free from a constant belief that God is evaluating me. I'm tired. I want to rest. The load is too heavy. I can't stand it." I would feel guilty for wanting this relief, especially when it crossed my mind that if I weren't a Christian, I wouldn't be living under this load of obligation. That very thought produced incredible guilt in me.

I lived under the dictum that "a sincere Christian tries hard." And I was sincere. This foundational belief created persistent pressure and anxiety. I assumed that stopping all my effort was tantamount to disappointing God. The problem is, of course, there will always be something more to do. There is never an end to it. I could never catch up. I could never find rest.

I wanted off this fear-driven treadmill with its relentless expectations, living as I was with the belief that I must "do my best for Jesus." This thinking was heavily influenced by a song I learned as a young child.

"Jesus wants me for a sunbeam to shine for him each day.

In every way try to please him. At home, at school, at play."

Living a life pleasing to God is certainly important (1 Thessalonians 4:1; Colossians 1:9b, 10). However, this occurs as a result of the work of the Holy Spirit's life through me, not by *my* effort. I only need to be *willing* for him to work in and through me. The only way to be released of the burden I placed on myself was to be enlightened by a good reason to operate differently—a reason grounded in truth.

In the following chapters, I will explain the underlying reasons behind my restlessness and how these points of tension were ultimately resolved.

Jesus Wants me for a Sunbeam (Nellie Talbot, music composed by Edwin O. Excell)

Jesus wants me for a sunbeam,
To shine for Him each day;
In every way try to please Him,
At home, at school, at play.

Refrain

A sunbeam, a sunbeam,
Jesus wants me for a sunbeam;
A sunbeam, a sunbeam,
I'll be a sunbeam for Him.

Jesus wants me to be loving,
And kind to all I see;
Showing how pleasant and happy
His little one can be.

I will ask Jesus to help me
To keep my heart from sin,
Ever reflecting His goodness,
And always shine for Him.

I'll be a sunbeam for Jesus;
I can if I but try
Serving Him moment by moment,
Then live with Him on high

Chapter 2

Chrysalis

Faith and Works

Apostle James says, "Don't you remember that our ancestor Abraham was shown to be right with God by his *actions* (italics mine) when he offered his son Isaac on the altar?" (James 2: 21). He continues, "You see, we are shown to be right with God by what we *do,* not by faith alone" (James 2:24, italics mine). The final point he brings home to the reader is "Just as the body is dead without breath, so also *faith is dead without good works"* (James 2:26, italics mine).

Yet, Paul says, "For it is by grace you have been saved, through faith-and this is not from yourselves, it is the gift of God-*not by works,* so that no one can boast" (Ephesians 2:8, 9, italics mine).

Paul and James seem to contradict each other.

So which is it, faith or works? Paul affirms I am "saved by grace and not of works." Yet, James seems to add a requirement for works. I reconciled these seeming dichotomies by believing that while salvation was by grace, God *did* want me to try to be a "good Christian." By this, I mean exerting a conscientious effort to living my life in such a way that would result in God's approval (i.e., works). To try hard was to show my devotion to God and that I was serious about living out my faith. This was foundational to the belief system that directed me. Indeed, the Bible *does* speak of effort and discipline (Colossians 3:23, 24; 1 Corinthians 9:25; Philippians 3:14; Colossians 1:28, 29). However, the *type* of effort I was engaged in defied both grace and faith.

Jesus says, "Not everyone who calls out to me 'Lord! Lord!' will enter the Kingdom of Heaven. Only those who actually do the will of my Father in heaven will enter" (Matthew 7:21). Don't those words indicate that works are important?

Seemingly contradictory are his words, "On judgement day many will say to me, 'Lord! Lord! We prophesied in your name and cast out demons in your name and performed many miracles in your name.' But I will reply, 'I never knew you. Get away from me, you who break God's laws'" (Matthew 7:22, 23).

So on one hand, it seems that if you don't do the will of the Father, you won't enter the kingdom. On the other hand, some who did all sorts of works for Jesus will be told by him to leave his presence because he never knew them.

This was really confusing for me.

And then there was ground zero: Abraham. Abraham was the man God commanded to actually sacrifice his own son to prove his love for him. It doesn't get worse than that. This example seemed to demonstrate conclusively that God wants evidence of devotion—*doing* something to show you love God.[2] But how much do you have to *do*, and what might God require of you as

---

[2] See Appendix: Abraham

adequate proof? How would you know? What does God want?

God gave the prophet, Micah, the answer to this question: "What can we bring to the Lord? What kind of offerings should we bring him?" (Micah 6:6a). In his response to the Israelites' suggestions, we discover God does not demand or desire sacrifices and offerings. He wants more than that—something far better and more important than all the *things* we could bring.

"The Lord has told you what is good, and this is what he requires of you: to do what is right, to love mercy, and to walk humbly with your God" (Micah 6:8).

Of all the possible requirements God could have given, he tells Micah it is justice, mercy, and humility he most desires. God prefers these three qualities to any tangible offering or service we could perform. What does it mean to walk humbly? It is to live in dependence on God. He wants me to love the things he loves: justice and kindness. He wants to create in me a longing for these things in my inner self, where my will and desires are, from which my decisions originate. I will call this the heart. The heart is what God wants above all else—above my best and most noble *efforts* to live a Christian life.

But what of works? Works are certainly a vital part of the life of a Christian as James asserts. They show that faith is alive. However, when James says faith without works is dead, he is not putting out a call to get to work and start doing things. He is not saying "Faith without *trying hard* is dead." "Trying hard" is not what he means by "works." James is not saying I try to prove my faith is genuine by *doing works*.

Doing something to prove your faith is alive makes works the priority, rather than the heart. I could do works for a myriad of reasons that have nothing to do with loving God or others (Proverbs 16:2). Jesus called the Pharisees "white-washed tombs" (Matthew 23:27, 28). They were all appearance and show. Despite their beliefs (faith) and trying to live righteously through good works and rule-keeping, they had no life within them. They were correct to a fault, but they did not love God.

When Christ has my heart, my faith is far more than just intellectual—important as the intellect is to faith. When faith is more than intellectual, faith is alive because it is animated by the Holy Spirit. Faith that is alive *will* produce good works. Christ works through me, and the works I do are prompted by his Spirit. The "good works, which God prepared in advance for us to do" (Ephesians 2:10) are the inevitable consequence of a heart that is given to Christ.

A heart given to Christ is open (not closed) to what he wants to say to you about yourself. An open heart is willing to let Christ live his life through you. This willingness gives permission to the Holy Spirit to transform your thoughts and attitudes, giving rise to actions that are spontaneously motivated by the Holy Spirit, produced by faith, and prompted by love (1 Thessalonians 1:3).

I realized it is not a matter of me trying to think about the works I need to produce to show my faith is not dead. My works demonstrate (prove) my faith insofar as a heart that is given to Christ will automatically produce them by virtue of the Spirit working in me

(Philippians 2:13). This is the "well of living water" Jesus speaks of (John 4:10). The heart *must* precede the doing. A faith that recognizes the grace of God, a faith imbued by the Holy Spirit, is a living faith that produces works. They occur as I live with flexibility and a willingness to be directed. A Christ-centred heart produces works, but *works do not produce a Christ-centred heart.*

James challenges those who say that they believe only intellectually (a dead faith) toward a faith that is truly alive. How does faith become alive? It is completely the work of the Holy Spirit. It is a faith that invites the Spirit of God to make his home in you, to abide. It is a faith that comes from being rooted in Christ—a faith that will spontaneously generate works. Works don't necessarily demonstrate that faith is alive, but an alive faith will always produce works.

The problem was I did not grasp how far the grace of God extends. God had never been asking me to prove the sincerity of my faith through what I did, which was the source of my struggle and agitation.

I found the answer to my question concerning faith and works in the following verse: "You see his [Abraham's] faith and actions worked together. His actions made his faith complete" (James 2:22). I finally understood. The seeming conflict between faith and works was wonderfully resolved. Abraham's faith was a living faith. He trusted in God's promises. From there he acted.

"Abraham *believed* God and God counted him righteous because of his faith" (Romans 4:3, italics mine). Abraham's faith saved him, not his works. His works were the consequence of his faith. So it is with those who trust in Christ. We believe in his promise to save fully and completely. And the indwelling Holy Spirit does his works through us.

James and Paul do not contradict each other. Salvation is entirely by grace, not by works; it is not attained through effort. It is expressed in works that are motivated by love as the Holy Spirit lives the life of Christ through the one who possesses a living faith.

Two Kinds of Faith

There are two kinds of faith: a living, Christ-rooted faith from which works flow spontaneously, or simply an intellectual faith. Intellectually, the Devil himself believes (James 2:19). Therefore, belief can be entirely unrelated to the indwelling of the Holy Spirit.

Unless you have more than intellectual assent to history (the death and resurrection of Christ), unless you have given Christ your *self*, your faith is dead. Dead intellectual faith cannot do the Father's will because the heart has not been given to Christ.

A heart given to Christ is where life is. It is a living faith. A living faith is an openness for Christ to transform your will, concerns, and desires to reflect his. The works that James refers to are entirely initiated by the Holy Spirit. There is a paradox in this. There is effort; yet, they are effortless—works and rest coexisting. Works, while demonstrating that faith is alive, are not an exercise in trying to prove it is. This is a crucial distinction. Instead of living a life of energy-consuming striving, you live in freedom. The spontaneous outpouring of works comes from the Christ source deep within. The Spirit leads; he does not push or pressure. You feel as if you are joyfully gliding as opposed to being propelled by fear. These works are energy-producing. They are the result of God being at work in you, giving you the desire and power to do what pleases him as you cooperate with the Spirit's prompting. It is an energy beyond yourself that is rooted in God's power. It is Christ living in you (Colossians 1:27, 29; Philippians 2:13).

The Message Bible translates Philippians 2:13 like this: "Be energetic in your life of salvation, reverent and sensitive before God. That energy is *God's* energy, an energy deep within you, God himself willing and working at what will give him the most pleasure" (italics mine).

As I give Christ my *self*, I open a space within which the Holy Spirit can cultivate his fruit of love, joy, peace, patience, kindness, goodness, faithfulness, gentleness, and self-control. This fruit is Christ-likeness and is possible because of the indwelling presence of the Holy Spirit. It is expressed in how I live life, impacting my interactions with others and all my activities. These activities are typically thought of as "works." However, the *fruit* God establishes and nurtures in me *is the work*. The evidence of this work of God is expressed naturally through love as Christ makes his desires mine. The presence of the fruit of the Spirit motivates what I do; the impetus originates from what Christ has done in me. This is "his mighty power at work" (Ephesians 3:20). What I do arises as I abide in Christ. As I give the Holy Spirit permission to develop the qualities of Jesus in me, my life will outwardly reflect the work he is accomplishing internally (Romans 8:29).

Christ is the vine (John Chapter 15). Life flows from the vine and provides nourishment for the branches, which, in turn, produce the fruit. It is through connection to the vine that I am open to receiving his life flow (John 15:4).

The fruit of the Spirit and the demonstration of it are not separate; they are entirely integrated. I don't need to try to prove the fruit is there by what I do. That would be putting the focus on my effort. The Spirit transforms me, and from there I act. Works done apart from the fruit of the Spirit are arduous. They are characterized by "I have to" or "I need to." By contrast, activities and interactions that flow from the fruit of the Spirit are joyous. They are propelled by a life-giving impetus behind them. This is deeply liberating.

Abiding

Jesus says that in coming to him and learning from him, I will find rest in the deepest part of my being. This requires abiding. It is a place where I can cease striving. Be still (Psalm 46:10).

I didn't know how to do this.

When I was a child at summer camp, I learned the hymn "Abide with Me." Each evening, a chorus of women and girls joined in acapella harmony around a crackling fire at our vocal benediction.

"Fast falls the eventide." The glowing embers of the coals. "The darkness deepens." The sun gently set into the horizon, casting a golden light across the Pacific Ocean.

"Help of the helpless, O abide with me." The dark embers gently flew away in the evening breeze.

Peace and stillness reigned and filled my heart as together we affirmed the love of our heavenly Father.

He abides with us. We abide in him.

What does it mean to abide? I have come to understand that abiding means to be fully present with God. When I abide in Christ, there is no hiding. God knows me intimately anyway. I embrace total honesty with my joys, fears, confusion, impatience, and anger. All of it. And Christ takes this gift and meets me where I am. I once thought I could not be as forthcoming with every untidy bit of me. I wasn't able to fully disclose everything I thought and felt because I often believed what I thought and felt was wrong. I couldn't imagine I could talk these things over with God. But I can. I have discovered it is through transparency that I find the acceptance which has existed all along.

Abiding is rest without anxiety. It is drawing from the Source of life. It is a place of trust, and with trust comes peace. It is letting the nourishment in the vine,

Christ himself, fill me with the life of the Spirit; from this filling, I can give to others.

To abide means to receive from the Christ-vine and let him feed my soul with his truth. It is to be open and receptive. It is not about trying to feel something spiritual. It is wanting reciprocal sharing—my heart with God and his heart with mine. I open myself to Scripture and let it penetrate. I am ready to hear what the Holy Spirit may wish to impress upon me. In quietness, I am willing to wait for this. Sometimes, the Holy Spirit animates Scripture in a deeply personal way, but other times, he remains silent. I come with no preconceived expectations or goals other than to be still. I simply expose myself to God's Word.

Inevitably, prayer lives in the practice of abiding. I simply place myself before God. I might speak to him aloud or express myself silently when words are deficient.

Apostle Paul says to pray all the time (1 Thessalonians 5:17). This is not a matter of simply saying words or having a designated quiet time, but rather maintaining a posture of attentiveness to and dialogue with the Lord throughout the day. It is simply knowing you are living in the presence of God.

There is peace, security, and trust when abiding. Christ gives me peace. He speaks truth. The truth sets me free (John 8:32). Abiding is a place without fear. It is a place of growth and rest.

Chapter 3

Emergence

Into the Light

Although I affirmed the grace of God, I worried as if it didn't exist at all. I always wondered if I was meeting the degree of activity I thought God was expecting of me. Always anxious, I lived with an eye to what I thought I should be doing but wasn't. I was chronically conscious of my omissions.

There was never an end to potential involvements, people to call or visit, ministries to be part of, or places to support financially. I could never do everything. But how would I know if what I *was* doing was sufficient? In making choices, was I neglecting something more important? How did God feel about me if I was? I believed in a God who was constantly demanding something from me, and who I was never quite sure was pleased with the effort I was making.

Then came the wonderful moment, a literal moment as I was driving up a hill on the way home. The Holy Spirit revealed to me that *works are the inevitable consequence of a heart given fully to Christ.* I felt smacked by a reality that astounded and astonished me. I realized I didn't need to worry about if I'm doing enough. These works I was so worried about doing, the Holy Spirit would accomplish. Suddenly, I was free. Just like that. A light switched on, and the fear that drove me vanished.

For many months, I had been physically unable to be consumed with anxiety-ridden self-preoccupation, so I was beginning to experience what rest felt like. But now, I knew for sure I did not need to take on this burden ever again; there was no reason to. It felt almost unbelievable.

I had paid attention to the "work out your salvation" part in Philippians 2:12, but I missed the most crucial element: God at work in me (v.13). Over and over, I reflected on that incredible paradigm shift in my thinking. God is at work in me through his Holy Spirit. "For God is at work." I am not on my own living out my salvation. He is within me, helping me, guiding me.

James finally made sense. I was no longer confused. Works are important, but it is God who is doing them as he expresses his love for others through me (Romans 5:5). It is the result of a living (not dead intellectual) faith. I discovered, to my joy, that there was no bar of achievement to reach after all. There was nothing to be stressed about. The tension between grace and works was wonderfully resolved. The grace of God not only saves me from sin but also fulfills the works aspect of the Christian life that James writes about.

I can trust God's activity in my life. I felt as if a heavy curtain was pulled back that let the sunshine in. I was fully liberated from my fear of not doing enough or trying hard enough. I was freed from trying to measure my achievements. For the first time in my life, I felt what it was like to live unselfconsciously as opposed to being emotionally drained by what I thought I should be accomplishing. Gone were the oppressive "shoulds" and "musts." I had no idea how much living under the weight of those two words tired me out emotionally and spiritually.

I have come to understand that giving of my *self* to Christ is more important to him than my service. What God desires is not things I've *done* or my *efforts* to try to please him, but my heart. That is what he wants first and foremost. God can then infuse me with his spirit, resulting in a spontaneous flow of good works free from the burden of obligation. They are the inevitable consequence of being open to the life of Christ working in and through me.

"Not trying" is not inactivity. Far from it. After the pressure I had been living under lifted, I found I was involved in the lives of others, but it was energy-producing, instead of energy-consuming. I felt no internal pressure to serve. There were no works to keep track of, no insecurity in thinking what I was doing might be inadequate. It dawned on me that everything Jesus did was guided by the Father and empowered by the Holy Spirit. He wasn't anxious like I was. He wasn't acting from a sense of obligation or a need to earn approval. Jesus said to learn from him. He said that by doing so I would find rest. He asked those who were weary and carrying heavy burdens to come to him (Matthew 11:28-30). That was me. I finally put them down and have learned how to live in the same joy-filled, Spirit-motivated freedom as Christ.

Freedom

Jesus said, "You will know the truth, and the truth will set you free" (John 8:32).

It is because of the truth of Scripture that my thinking has been radically changed. Restructured. The lies I told myself were "fiery arrows," which have been extinguished through faith (Ephesians 6:16). I am now free from the constriction of fear. Fear is an obstruction and impediment to seeing the life-giving realities found in truth.

I trust Christ to live his life through me with *exactly* the same dependency as I trust his work on the cross. The Christian life is entered into by grace; it is similarly lived out by the same grace (Colossians 2:6, 7). God desires that I trust him to save me wholly and completely. Salvation is both past and present tense; it is both a finished act and a journey. It is what Christ has done for me and what he is doing in and through me.

It is actually as a consequence of my reliance on him that the power of the Holy Spirit is released (2 Corinthians 12:8, 9). So the greatest challenge in the Christian life is to stay dependent. The process toward Christ-likeness is never a matter of willpower, resolutions, or trying to prove devotion to God through works.

Freedom has come as I have grasped that God isn't keeping track of what I do and doling out points. There is no scale where my works outweigh my lack of them. I have been liberated from the notion of an elusive bar that I feared I was being judged against. I do not need to "try hard to do." Christ wasn't focused on himself, attempting to gain approval from the Father by the things he did. He had the Father's approval. And I have the same approval in Christ. In him, I have "measured up." I no longer carry the burden of thinking my best efforts may not be sufficient.

Performance isn't required. This truth has made all the difference. By faith, I can walk into a place of rest.

I discovered, to my relief, that I was my own slave driver; it wasn't God who was driving me. Christ's desire is not that I live under the weightiness and unrelenting tyranny of "shoulds," but that I give him a heart he can work with. It is the orientation of my heart toward him that he cares about; that is all.

Therefore, I can remove the pressure from myself. Becoming is a process, initiated and sustained by Christ. What I *can* do is simply show up. Paul calls this "presenting yourself" (Romans 12:1). Like Isaiah, I just tell God that I am here and available (Isaiah 6:8).

The works I do are because the Holy Spirit lives in and through me. As I said earlier, works are the inevitable consequence of a living faith and are activated by him. The Holy Spirit works in my life, which results in "doing." There is nothing for me to be proud of (Romans 3:27). As a matter of fact, anything I do for God is actually God's gift to *me*. I get to be a participant in what he is doing in the lives that intersect with mine—in my family, community, and throughout the world. The love of God within compels action; you cannot help expressing this love in practical ways.

I cannot hold up a single thing to merit God's approval. Grace is the antithesis of achievement. I can do absolutely nothing to qualify for God's grace or to be accepted by him. There is nothing to add to the finished work of the cross and resurrection. There is only the cannot-be-earned love and grace of God. He is Saviour from start to finish. I rely entirely on the sufficiency of Jesus. "Working out" salvation does not mean adding my works to secure what Christ has already accomplished.

Resting in the grace of Christ, and understanding its implications, I am now able to live joyfully without tension. I have peace (1 John 4:16-18). I come to him empty-handed. No "look what I've done for you." There is much joy in that. Fear of not measuring up is dispelled. I am released from a burdensome focus on myself. Fear no longer lurks in the shadows subconsciously prompting my actions. I now live with a freeing self-forgetfulness.

This is what I know: God saves me entirely by his grace. He works in and through me by his grace. It is all a gift.

Rest

"I will give you rest" (Matthew 11:28). If I am trying hard, I can't experience the grace of God—him working through me, which sets me free to rest. For rest is what Christ invites his followers to. And from what does he offer rest if not from our efforts, works, and strivings? This is the burden he wishes to take from us. "Come to me," he says.

Instead of paying attention to my "doing," I can just *be*. I can rest from trying to prove something. I give myself to God. Like Isaiah, I say, "Here I am." God sends, and I have the joy of going. Like the widow in the temple (Mark 12:41-44; Luke 21:1-4) and the giver of the cup of water (Matthew 10:42), I may never be cognizant of the significance of the gift. When I open myself to be propelled by the Spirit, he fills me with his desires and concerns. The desire to give to others, the desire to pray, the desire to worship, the desire to focus on the words in Scripture—it all comes from God himself.

The motivation given by the life of Christ within me enables the "doing" because of my response to God's love for me, resulting in the subsequent out-flowing of his love for others. He can spark my imagination and lead me into areas of service, the impact of which I may be unaware. The energy is derived from him. The recognition and commendation of others are irrelevant. This is very freeing.

As I continue to be receptive to what God would say to me, he motivates my actions. This realization was the key that unlocked the door to the great, vast place where I could truly breathe and run—released from the constricted, fearful space I occupied. I left behind the anxiety that bred self-consciousness and self-absorption as I came to understand the grace of God more fully and the role of the Holy Spirit in a life lived by faith, expressed through loving action.

Crucially, my spiritual growth depends not on what *I* do, but what I permit *God* to do through me. I expose myself to Scripture and let it permeate. Worship takes me beyond myself to the overarching reality of God. I pour myself out in prayer to him who knows me intimately and—incredibly—prays for me (Romans 8:26). This is not *trying*. This is not an *effort*. This is being present.

The grace of God anchors me. I come back to it time and time again.

- I am saved by grace and not by my works.
- I cannot do for myself what only God can do.
- I believe that just as I cannot accomplish my own salvation from sin, I cannot accomplish my own journey to Christ-likeness through my own endeavors. I live in dependency on him for everything.

I grow and serve by God's mercy—his promise to never leave or forsake me, and to extend his grace as he works in and through me. At a time of great weakness and inability to *do* anything, God's commitment to me was firm and unwavering. I discovered that by entering into rest, I am unencumbered, free from trying to accomplish the work of the Holy Spirit myself, and free from fearing the consequence of "unmet expectations." I experience peace. He is here. He is working. He is faithful.

Chapter 4

Final Word

Love

Now I come full circle to the first sentence of the Introduction. The most important implication of learning to rest in grace is that it enables you to better live in love. God is love. He is the source of love. He acts in love. Therefore, to be Christ-like is to love.

I realized to the degree that I am motivated by fear is the extent to which I cannot act from love. And works done from a reason other than love are *self*, rather than *other*-centered. They lack that fundamental essence that makes an action truly meaningful. Paul says that even if you give up your body to be burned, works are of no benefit if love is not the foundation (1 Corinthians 13:1-3). Giving up your body is the ultimate sacrifice, but if the motivation isn't love, what does it matter? Absolutely nothing, apparently.

God places value, not on the behaviour itself, but on the impetus behind it. Two acts might seem identical, but stem from entirely different motives. God can see the difference; the outward appearance doesn't matter (1 Samuel 16:7b).

Jesus' contrast between the Pharisees and the widow in the temple (Mark 12:44; Luke 21:3) indicates that he wants faith and love to be the only reasons for giving, for our works. Any amount given in that spirit is sufficient.

Fear squeezes out love. I was afraid of disappointing what I thought God wanted of me, so I lived a performance-oriented life. I also feared the judgement of others. So I often tried to protect myself from potential judgement by meeting perceived (real or not) expectations. Eventually it dawned on me that by doing so, I was not acting from love, but from fear and pressure. The only way to clear the way for love to motivate is to be free from fear. It is the only way to be truly honest in relationships and with oneself.

Understanding grace liberated me from the fear of judgement, making it possible for love to more fully influence my actions. Love displaces fear. When fear is gone, love is all that remains. This is expressed by the words of Apostle John:

> God is love. When we take up permanent residence in a life of love, we live in God and God lives in us. This way, love has the run of the house, becomes at home and mature in us so that we're free of worry on Judgment Day—our standing in the world is identical with Christ's. There is no room in love for fear. Well-formed love banishes fear. Since fear is crippling, a fearful life— fear of death, fear of judgment—is one not fully formed in love. (1 John 4: 16-18 The Message)

Jesus said that the truth will set you free. The truth of God's Word has done exactly that. It changed me. My freedom is grounded in the grace of God. I have continually brought this to mind over these many years since first penning my journal. As I trust in this grace and abide in him who is my spiritual life source, works inevitably flow *because of the power of the Holy Spirit* within me. These works cannot help but be expressed through love. It is the only thing that matters (Galatians 5:6).

Post-script

The struggles I have written about were not the cause of my illness. They are unrelated. However, when I became well, I could not live under the weight of any mental stress whatsoever. It was during this time of recovery that God showed me the burden I had been living under prior to becoming sick and how to be free of it. I have never once taken that burden upon myself again.

Throughout the following four to five years, I developed new habits of the mind. To accomplish this transition from one way of thinking to another, I needed anchoring to keep me from drifting back to familiar patterns, and Scripture provided that. The following passage became particularly important to me:

> I tell you the truth, anyone who sneaks over the wall of a sheepfold, rather than going through the gate, must

> surely be a thief and a robber! But the one who enters through the gate is the shepherd of the sheep. The gatekeeper opens the gate for him, and the sheep recognize his voice and come to him. He calls his own sheep by name and leads them out. After he has gathered his own flock he walks ahead of them, and they follow him because they know his voice. **They won't follow a stranger; they will run from him because they don't know his voice.** (John 10:1-5, bold mine)

The "voice of the stranger" for me were the words "You are not a good Christian if you don't...." Another was "You haven't (fill in the activity) enough." Or "You should...." Or "You haven't...." I am now fully aware that these condemning voices were not from Christ. They were the voices of the "stranger," so I did not have to listen. I learned to ignore them. If I ever felt accused of not "measuring up," or felt guilty about my inadequacies, I knew it was not the Lord. If

I felt pressured into works at the risk of displeasing God, I knew it was not he who was speaking. Over time, as I responded with the truth of Scripture and refused to listen to the "stranger's" voice, it became dimmer and dimmer. "The truth will set you free" (John 8:32). And it did.

Appendix

- Abraham
- Achievement and Self-Worth
- Christ, My Righteousness
- Conviction and Condemnation
- Romans 8:28
- Wisdom

Thought Anchors

Scripture References

Abraham

Abraham's sacrifice of Isaac scared me. I thought the point of this narrative was that I needed to be willing to lose what was most precious to me to demonstrate my love for God. Believing this made me afraid of what God might require. I could not understand how a loving God would deliberately cause me grief by asking me to prove something to him. I felt guilty because I realized it would be impossible for me to truly love God if I resented him for placing such demands on me. I could not resolve this formidable tension. However, this story is not about a test to see whether Abraham loved God more than he loved his son, Isaac; the point is about *faith*. In being willing to sacrifice Isaac, Abraham was demonstrating his belief in God's promise to bless him with descendants (Genesis 15:4, 5).

In the face of God's perplexing directive, Abraham still believed what God said he would do, and God declared Abraham to be righteous because of his faith (Genesis 15:6). Abraham's logical response could have been to question how God was ever going to give him descendants through Isaac as he had promised to do through Sarah's child, the child of the promise (Genesis 17:19). God's instruction to sacrifice this long-awaited son made absolutely no sense. In sheer confusion, Abraham could have told God he didn't believe his promise that there would be descendants through Isaac; a dead son can't have children. Or he could have refused to sacrifice Isaac to preserve his line of succession. But Abraham trusted God, believing that he would bring Isaac to life again (Hebrews 11:19). He even told his two servants that after he and Isaac had worshipped, *they* would come back (Genesis 22:5). God had promised descendants through Isaac, and Abraham believed it.

The test God gave Abraham concerned the extent to which Abraham *believed the promise*. And the fulfillment of the promise was based on God's integrity. Abraham had confidence in the truthfulness of God's promise and his ability to fulfill it (Romans 4:20, 21). He believed Isaac could be resurrected. He trusted in God's character and trustworthiness. Abraham's faith and subsequent obedience to this strange command demonstrated his love for God. He believed him.

This is why God could say to Abraham, "Now I know that you love me because you didn't withhold from me your only son" (Genesis 22:12).

Where there is love, there is trust; where there is trust, there is love.

God wanted to know that Abraham *loved* him; however, giving up/sacrificing something to God isn't necessarily proof of love. Abraham could have sacrificed Isaac with absolutely no love in his heart for God at all. He could have been angry. He could have been fearful of the consequences if he did not obey the command. But God wanted more than the mere following of orders. Obedience alone does not signify trust and love. You can obey orders without loving.

God doesn't want obedience alone. He doesn't care about worship when our hearts are distant from him (Matthew 15:7, 8; Isaiah 29:13). He doesn't desire empty rituals or resentful fear-induced compliance. He desires his love for us to be returned. It starts with God. He is the initiator of love. Abraham's obedient response to God was anchored in God's character.

Abraham had trust and confidence in God, and it was *that* which God was pleased with.

Abraham is the evidence that God desires faith above works (Romans Chapter 4). Actions alone do not necessarily spring from faith and love for God; they may arise from the motivation of fear. Obedience from the root of *fear* is antithetical to obedience from *love*.

Obedience prompted by love is entirely different from fear-based obedience. It is freedom. I obey because I trust. And I trust because I love. And I love because I am loved.

God is not asking me to do something painful to demonstrate my love for him. The centrality of the Old and New Testaments is that God loves. That God can be trusted. Having grasped that fully, I am no longer afraid.

Achievement and Self-worth

As I gradually recovered from being unwell, I lived in a brand new paradigm: I couldn't try to achieve anything. And for the first time in my life, I didn't care. I was just glad to be healthy again. I required a lot of rest, and I had my small child to spend time with. That was enough for me.

I came to the novel realization that my value as a person didn't diminish one bit by doing "nothing." Therefore, I concluded that the opposite is true: accomplishment doesn't add to my value. And if my value isn't altered according to what I do or don't do, then it follows I do not need to achieve to build my self-esteem. If achievement is unrelated to my self-esteem, so is failure. I have nothing to gain or lose by either. I am loved by God. He created me. I am of intrinsic value. This had huge implications for me going forward.

Eventually, I decided to help out with the youth group at church, and later, I returned to work part-time. I noticed I felt different. I wasn't trying to prove something to myself or anyone else, and I'd never experienced that before. It was no longer important to be perceived as conscientious or capable. I was able to be observant of my performance without being critical of myself. Who I considered myself to be wasn't determined or affected by what I accomplished. My self-esteem became detached from it. It was very freeing, and I was able to enjoy my work much more.

I also discovered something else during that time of necessary rest. Most things of value cannot even be measured. How do you measure reading and playing with a child, going for a walk in the forest, or listening to a friend pour out her heart?

Once I went back to work, I became less task-orientated in my off-hours. It became far less important to tick off items on a checklist in the comfort of my own home. At this point you might be asking how on earth a working person is supposed to live without ticking off boxes. I absolutely had a checklist and obligations to fulfill when I was working as a teacher. Furthermore, I have continued to tutor privately, taken courses, and have led classes for English Language Learners at my church while officially retired; these involvements naturally come with "have to" lists. The point is that I have learned how to balance work and relaxation, and have released myself from creating obligations for myself where none exist.

I am now able to make welcome room for valuable moments that cannot be measured. I prioritize these times over "getting things done." Doing a mental inventory of my day to feel as if I've accomplished something isn't consequential now. The daily "have dones" no longer have the power to make me feel good about myself. This has enabled me to better respond to whatever comes my way unexpectedly. They aren't "interruptions" in the way they used to be, meaning stopping me from what I was trying to get done at the time.

I have come to appreciate my value simply for who I am. Full stop. My accomplishments no longer validate me. I have learned not to let my achievements give me what God has already given and can never be taken away.

Christ, My Righteousness

I have said that God is not placing demands on me. But that is only partly true. In reality, there are plenty of expectations associated with Christian living. God says, "Be holy, as I am holy" (1 Peter 1:16). There are many "dos" and "do nots." There are the demands of the Sermon on the Mount. There is the goal of demonstrating love, joy, peace, patience, kindness, goodness, faithfulness, gentleness, and self-control (Galatians 5:22, 23). And who can, independent of Christ, live a life of love as depicted in 1 Corinthians Chapter 13? It feels impossible to attain. And it is.

However, the expectation God is *not* placing on me is to fulfill these lofty ideals on my own. This is a weight I am not meant to take on. Attempts to do so will always be met with failure. I cannot establish my righteousness apart from Christ. But, thank God, he *became* my righteousness (2 Corinthians 5:21). In Christ, I have measured up. I cannot do anything to make him approve of me more. I am "free from the law of sin and death" (Romans 8:2), which evaluates me against the holiness of God of which I fall short. There are no demands to meet in my own strength because Christ meets them, and I am in Christ. He gave his life for me, and I live my life by faith in him (Galatians 2:20).

Jesus does not place a heavy burden on his children. He wants me to come to him in every way so he can do for me what I am unable to do for myself. I come to the cross for salvation, and likewise rely on him to help me become more like Christ. The Christian life becomes burdensome when I see myself as the one who must accomplish this. But Christ lives his life through me by the power of the Holy Spirit. Philippians 2:12, 13 says to "work out your salvation," but this process is *only* possible because "It is God who works in you to *will* and to *act* according to his good purpose" (Philippians 2:13, italics mine). Because God is at work, I can relinquish to Christ the futility of trying to bring about through self-reliance that which I cannot. As Watchman Nee says,

> *It is God which worketh in you.* Deliverance from law does not mean that we are free from doing the will of God. It certainly does not mean that we are lawless. Very much the reverse! What it does mean however is that we are free from doing that will *as of ourselves.* (Nee, Watchman, *A Normal*

Christian Life, pg 111. Welch Publishing Company Inc., n.d.)

If salvation from sin and the ability to live a holy life were possible to attain myself, there would have been no need for Christ to die. It is a contradiction to acknowledge my sin, accept Christ's gift of forgiveness by grace, and then assume I am now responsible to live out the Christian life through my own effort. "*Just as* you trusted Christ to save you, live in union with him" (Colossians 2:6, italics mine). I am both saved and nourished by him.

The good news of the gospel is that I am free from trying to pull myself up notch by notch as if by doing so the disparity between myself and the glory of God could be reduced. There is no place for self-reliance or haughtiness. Christ is sufficient to bear my sin, reconcile me to God, and nurture the life-long process of increasing his qualities in my attitudes and actions as I invite him to do so. Salvation and the capacity to live a life that pleases God is all by faith in what he has done (completed), and what he will do in me through the presence and power of the Holy Spirit (ongoing). Both are gifts, not a matter of personal achievement.

I can never arrive at holiness through conscientious determination. I can practice new, positive habits, but the development of the fruit of the Spirit is a gift of his grace. He then gives me the ability and opportunity to do his works.

Obedience is not a pressure-filled obligation precisely because God gives me his Holy Spirit who fulfills what he desires. His activity in me sets me free to rest and depend on him. This surely is grace, and I am incredibly grateful.

Conviction and Condemnation
"Investigate my life, O God, find out everything about me; cross-examine and test me, get a clear picture of what I'm about; See for yourself whether I've done anything wrong—and guide me on the road to eternal life" (Psalm 139:23 24 The Message).

I used to feel guilty a lot, but I could never pinpoint the source of my guilt. There was just an underlying anxiety that I wasn't adequately meeting the expectations I believed God was placing on me. I didn't know how to recognize the difference between what *God* was telling me and what I was telling myself.

Jesus said his sheep know his voice, and they will not follow a stranger (John 10:2-5). The key for me was to learn how to discern Jesus' voice from my own. Scripture gives this enlightenment.

Firstly, Satan is referred to as an accuser (Revelation 12:10). Secondly, salvation means I am not under condemnation (Romans 8:1). Thirdly, I am saved by grace, not by effort or achievement (Ephesians 2:8). If I sense a weighty, finger-pointing "you," I know I am not hearing the voice of Christ, and I do not need to listen to it.

Condemnation makes me feel guilty with no way out. I feel accused and under a heavy burden. I find myself driven into works to compensate for my failings, none of which is enough to rescue me from sinking into a place of feeling profound failure and discouragement.

Unhealthy guilt propels one *away* from God into hopelessness. The result is a feeling of rejection that leads to self-loathing. By contrast, the conviction of the Holy Spirit leads me *toward* God into receiving forgiveness and grace. Through conviction, God reveals the truth. He uncovers those attitudes and actions that are ultimately destructive to me and impact others negatively. I then give them to God in a brutally honest confession with gratitude and hope. God wants to heal me. He wants to bring me into deep peace as opposed to guilt-ridden restlessness.

Condemnation drives us into works; conviction leads us into grace.

When God convicts me, I enter a spacious place of forgiveness and freedom that I didn't know was there. When God convicts, he pulls back the blinders, and I see myself more clearly. In doing so, God assures me I can come to him and embrace authenticity and transparency without fear. The revelations of God are gently penetrating and absolutely accurate. They hit the nail on the head. Self-deception is exposed for what it is and the harm it does.

If I say I am open to the conviction of the Holy Spirit, I must maintain a receptive heart; lack of receptiveness dulls the Spirit's voice. I must be willing to listen and heed. No self-justification or rationalization. No excuses. No pride. No defensiveness. No hiding. I must be willing to accept a picture of reality. I must choose to acknowledge the truth of what God shows me, though I may be inclined to resist. I must choose to walk in the light (1 John 1:7). I acknowledge and embrace the unpleasant truth about myself, but am aware of the hope of healing, restoration, and renewal. If I am closed to what Christ would say, then I limit the extent to which he can work in and through me.

It is important to assess myself accurately (Romans 12:3). I must be willing to hear what God has to say and make positive directional changes in my way of thinking and behaving. This about-face often involves, where possible, taking a step toward restoration with another and asking for forgiveness.

In revealing my sin to me, the Holy Spirit's intention is not to make me feel like a failure. God does not want me to try harder or do better so he can approve of me more. He does not want me to redouble my efforts in shame. Quite the contrary. Confessing (admitting) the truth that I do not love perfectly as Christ does, makes me so grateful for the cross of Christ and the pardon made possible through his self-sacrifice.

Reflecting on an awareness that comes courtesy of the Spirit is life-giving. It is like opening the window and breathing fresh air. I gain release from hindrances and know the guidance and power are there to embrace and live in something better. Discouragement gives way to hope and transformation. It leads me to God and the reality that I am loved and forgiven. That is where my identity lies. I simply trust that God will reveal in his way and time what I need to be aware of. Deep assurance of the love and faithfulness of God makes this possible.

Romans 8:28

When he was 18 years old, my husband had an accident that resulted in the amputation of his right forearm. I met him four years later. Gord was told by a well-meaning individual that maybe God allowed this accident to happen to draw him nearer to God. Since

God is sovereign, the man reasoned God must have permitted Gord to experience this life-altering tragedy for some purpose. This is probably not an uncommon conclusion of the verse "In all things God works for the good of those who love him, who have been called according to his purpose."

Early in our relationship, I asked Gord how he had dealt with such devastation in his life. He told me that he had given away his guitar because he no longer had any use for it. He abandoned his nascent music major, as he was unable to play his chosen instrument. His athletic interests and involvements were severely curtailed. All these years later, I will never forget the exact words he said to me: "I decided I could be bitter, or I could give it to God to work with."

That is what my husband did at the age of 18 with his life forever changed and formidable challenges ahead. It was not a "given" that Gord would have drawn closer to God. He could very well have lived the rest of his life in bitterness and self-pity. He could have blamed God for not preventing the accident—or in the words of some— "allowed" it. But Gord chose to reject all this, choosing instead, in his distress, myriad questions, and fear of what the future would hold for him, to lean into the Lord who loved him and also grieved the awfulness of what happened that August afternoon.

God does not dream up ways to bring hardship into someone's life in order to bring some good of it. I do not believe "everything happens for a reason." I do not search for meaning or an over-arching divine purpose to explain disappointment or loss. We live in a world where everyone is vulnerable to sickness, disease, accidents, financial loss, or any catastrophic event. The Christian is not exempt.

As this manuscript entered into its final phase before publication, my 34-year-old son-in-law died of brain cancer. There is nothing good about this; it can never be transformed into something good. Tragedy stands alone as tragedy.

Any good that comes of Brett's death will be despite, not because of it. This distinction is of crucial importance. The word "because" seeks for an answer.

The human mind searches for reasons. It wants to understand "why." It wants to believe that there was, after all, a hidden purpose that will provide meaning to a terrible experience. However, the word "despite," in this context is a note of sheer grace that gives no reason.

There can be no "reason" for my son-in-law's death that would ever bring me comfort. But I trust in the "despite." The insights that I have shared in this book have come *despite* my illness so long ago, not *because* of it. The maturity my husband gained in the years following his accident was *despite* what happened. God did not "allow" it *so that* Gord would learn something. If you think about it carefully, a belief that God would allow a tragedy for any "reason" is incompatible with a God of love.

Jesus promised that we would have "many trials and sorrows" (John 16:33 NLT). "But fear not...." The gift lies in the "but." That is where hope resides in the suffering of loss.

"You prepare a feast for me in the presence of my enemies," writes the psalmist (Psalm 23:5). No matter how hopeless or disappointed you may feel in your darkest moments, you have not been abandoned. Whatever "enemy" in my life and in yours will not have the last word. The good work of God does. God is the God of redemption in this fallen world with all its joys and sorrows. He is the God of the "despite."

Wisdom

"Send out your light and your truth; let them guide me" (Psalm 43:3).

I used to seek wisdom out of fear of making a mistake. Getting wisdom was a way for me to insulate and protect myself from things going wrong. I assumed that if I had God's wisdom, all would go smoothly. It was a kind of insurance policy against grief. Wisdom would enable me to do the "right" thing, which minimized risk. I didn't understand the purpose of wisdom any other way. I reasoned that God wouldn't give me wisdom and let things go sideways.

However, the goal of wisdom isn't simply to avoid making a wrong decision. Wisdom isn't all about being correct. The purpose of desiring wisdom is to become like Christ, as it is from a Christ-like mind that Christ-like decisions flow.

I am invited to ask for wisdom (James 1:5). Wisdom guards against the foolishness and destructiveness resulting from misguided or self-centered decisions or priorities. The book of Proverbs is full of caution. Decisions that are wise will have, among others, the qualities of purity, peace, consideration, and mercy. God gives his wisdom so that our choices express these attributes (James 3:17).

When I am receptive to the voice of the Holy Spirit, I am in a position to gain wisdom. Wisdom guides me in the way of love and truth.

When God gives wisdom, he is giving me the eyes of Jesus and sharing the mind of Christ (1 Corinthians 2:16). As I am conformed more and more to the image of Christ, I will be able to see more accurately. As I gain clarity from Christ's perspective, actions follow that originate in love. As I choose to be receptive and ask for wisdom to know Christ more, I will be better able to discern.

Prayer is crucial here. Prayer connects me to God, the transcendent Being who is the source of life and wisdom. Prayer is dependency. Dependency on God enables me to be more clear-sighted.

It is through openness in prayer that I can hear from the Spirit of God and reflect on what he reveals to me. Prayer keeps me grounded and humble; it guards against an inflated view of self (Romans 12:3). It is through open-hearted acceptance of the truth that I am protected from a tendency to block uncomfortable realities about myself.

I once made plans to move across the country. After the circumstances that prompted my decision altered, I began asking for wisdom regarding what to do. The option to leave town for another city closer to home was a possibility. However, God did not answer my prayers with a clear directive to stay or go. Simply following orders would not have enabled me to mature;

I would have learned absolutely nothing. But the truth, which is wisdom, changed me, and subsequently, my desires changed.

My prayers for guidance were answered, but differently than I expected. I became aware of my motivation to move in the first place; I understood myself better. With that knowledge, I decided to stay where I was. I saw the situation from Christ's perspective. The decision I made reflected the health and growth God wanted for me. That was and is the bottom line.

The prayers of "Where does God want me to live?" or "What does God want me to do for a vocation?" or "Where does God want me to go to school?" are questions that cause stress for many Christians because they seldom get clear-cut answers. I believe "Who am I becoming?" is the question God wants us to ask the most. My goal and desire are to grow in wisdom and the fruit of the Holy Spirit. No matter where I find myself circumstantially, these attributes can be developed within me by God's grace.

Appendix

Wisdom is about understanding, insight, and perception. It is a treasure (Proverbs 2:1-6). It is from this gift that decisions can be made, which protect, guard, and save. Emotionally and spiritually mature decisions are the result of seeking wisdom, but I am meant to do some thinking. The invitation to ask for wisdom isn't a matter of praying, "Tell me what to do so that I don't have to think about it at all."

Gaining wisdom is not simply a matter of waiting for instructions; it is about becoming the kind of person who is capable of discerning a wise path in which to walk. The decision is mine to take responsibility for. In some instances, a course of action is unambiguous; other times it is more nuanced. Gaining wisdom is about becoming more like Christ, which enables me to perceive and act accordingly. It is a life-long process.

When asking for wisdom, I no longer think I need to sit immobilized, stalled, and afraid to move forward. I no longer fear that God might not speak, or that I might have missed his guidance. I make decisions and am willing to remain flexible, adaptable, and receptive. I choose not to be rigid. I am prepared to change direction as I learn more about myself or a situation, most often with the wise counsel of those I trust.

The book of Proverbs, in particular, stresses the importance of humbly receiving the wisdom of others, gained through their experience and walk with God. You must be willing to listen and possibly alter or abandon your course, not stubbornly clinging to your own plans and perspective. Ways of receiving the valuable guidance of others can come, not only from conversations but also through books, sermons, podcasts, and other means of communication. We are not meant to go it alone. God has provided community.

God is with me on this journey of life and has provided the guidance of others as I grow and mature in faith and discernment. And he is merciful. I don't take a wrong turn and find him no longer there. I can't live with faith and freedom if I am consumed with fear and perfectionism. God is present in the biggest errors I could ever make. He has been with me in the mistakes I *have* made and will continue to make. Mistakes are not irredeemable. God takes and transforms them for my benefit. He works good for me all the time in everything (Romans 8:28). The Lord is redemptive; there is always hope and new beginnings.

Stumbling along the path of life, and learning along the way, leads to increased perception, self-awareness, and maturity. I can have peace that is born of trust in God's faithfulness, no matter what. The fear is gone.

Thought Anchors

- God is committed to me. I can trust him to:
  - speak to me
  - guide me
  - convict me

- There is nothing to add to the cross of Christ. Grace has no addition sign.

- God wants my heart and the presentation of myself first and foremost. That is all.

- Works are the inevitable consequence of a living faith—a heart given to Christ.

Scripture References (by chapter)

Introduction

- Surely the Lord was in this place, and I wasn't even aware of it. (Genesis 28:16 NLT)

- And we know that in all things God works for the good of those who love him, who have been called according to his purpose. (Romans 8:28 NIV)

Chapter 1 - Rear View

Faultlines

- Are you tired? Worn out? Burned out on religion? Come to me. Get away with me and you'll recover your life. I'll show you how to take a real rest. Walk with me and work with me—watch how I do it. Learn the unforced rhythms of grace. I won't lay anything heavy or ill-fitting on you. Keep company with me and you'll learn to live freely and lightly. (Matthew 11:28-30 The Message)

- As he thinks within himself, so is he. (Proverbs 23:7a NASB)

- For the Kingdom of God is not a matter of what we eat or drink, but of living a life of goodness and peace and joy in the Holy Spirit. (Romans 14:17)

Reconstruction

- What shall we say about such things? If God is for us, who can ever be against us? (Romans 8:31 NLT)

Burdened

- Finally, dear brothers and sisters, we urge you in the name of the Lord Jesus to live in a way that pleases God, as we have taught you. (1 Thessalonians 4:1 NLT)

- We ask God to give you complete knowledge of his will and to give you spiritual wisdom and understanding. Then the way you live will always honor and please the Lord, and your lives will produce every kind of good fruit. All the while, you will grow as you learn to know God better and better. (Colossians 1:9b, 10 NLT)

Chapter 2 - Chrysalis

Faith and Works

- Don't you remember that our ancestor Abraham was shown to be right with God by his actions when he offered his son Isaac on the altar? (James 2:21 NLT)

- You see, we are shown to be right with God by what we do, not by faith alone. (James 2:24 NLT)

- Just as the body is dead without breath, so also faith is dead without good works. (James 2:26 NLT)

- For it is by grace you have been saved, through faith -and this is not from yourselves, it is the gift of God--not by works, so that no one can boast. (Ephesians 2:8, 9 NIV)

- Work willingly at whatever you do, as though you were working for the Lord rather than for people. Remember that the Lord will give you an inheritance as your reward, and that the Master you are serving is Christ. (Colossians 3:23, 24 NLT)

- All athletes are disciplined in their training. They do it to win a prize that will fade away, but we do it for an eternal prize. (1 Corinthians 9:25 NLT)

- I press on to reach the end of the race and receive the heavenly prize for which God, through Christ Jesus is calling us. (Philippians 3:14 NLT)

Scripture References

- So we tell others about Christ, warning everyone and teaching everyone with all the wisdom God has given us. We want to present them to God, perfect in their relationship to Christ. That's why I work and struggle so hard, depending on Christ's mighty power that works within me. (Colossians 1:28, 29 NLT)

- Not everyone who calls out to me 'Lord! Lord!' will enter the Kingdom of Heaven. Only those who actually do the will of my Father in heaven will enter. (Matthew 7:21 NLT)

- "On judgement day many will say to me, 'Lord! Lord! We prophesied in your name and cast out demons in your name and performed many miracles in your name.' But I will reply, 'I never knew you. Get away from me, you who break God's laws.'" (Matthew 7:22, 23 NLT)

- What can we bring to the Lord? What kind of offerings should we give him? Should we bow before God with offerings of yearly calves? Should we offer him thousands of rams and ten thousand rivers of olive oil? Should we sacrifice our firstborn children to pay for our sins? No, O people, the Lord has told you what is good, and this is what he requires of you: to do what is right, to love mercy, and to walk humbly with your God. (Micah 6:6-8 NLT)

- People may be pure in their own eyes, but the Lord examines their motives. (Proverbs 16:2 NLT)

- What sorrow awaits you teachers of religious law and you Pharisees. Hypocrites! For you are like whitewashed tombs—beautiful on the outside but filled on the inside with dead people's bones and all sorts of impurity. Outwardly you look like righteous people, but inwardly your hearts are filled with hypocrisy and lawlessness. (Matthew 23:27, 28 NLT)

- For we are God's workmanship, created in Christ Jesus to do good works, which God prepared in advance for us to do. (Ephesians 2:10 NIV)

- We continually remember before our God and Father your work produced by faith, your labor prompted by love, and your endurance inspired by hope in our Lord Jesus Christ. (1 Thessalonians 1:3 NIV)

- For God is working in you, giving you the desire and power to do what pleases him. (Philippians 2:13 NLT)

- Jesus answered her [the Samaritan woman], "If you only knew the gift of God and who it is that asks you for a drink, you would have asked him and he would have given you living water." (John 4:10 NIV)

Scripture References

- You see, his faith and his actions worked together. His actions made his faith complete. (James 2:22 NLT)

- For the Scripture tells us, "Abraham believed God, and God counted him righteous because of his faith." When people work, their wages are not a gift, but something they have earned. But people are counted as righteous, not because of their work, but because of their faith in God who forgives sinners. (Romans 4:3-5 NLT)

Two Kinds of Faith
- You say you have faith because you believe there is one God. Good for you! Even the demons believe this, and they tremble in terror. (James 2:19 NLT)

- For God wanted them to know [God's people] that the riches and glory of Christ are for you Gentiles, too. And this is the secret: Christ lives in you. This gives you assurance of sharing his glory....That's why I work and struggle so hard, depending on Christ's mighty power that works within me. (Colossians 1:27, 29 NLT)

- For God is working in you, giving you the desire and the power to do what pleases him. (Philippians 2:13 NLT)

- Now all glory to God, who is able, through his mighty power at work within us, to accomplish infinitely more than we might ask or think. (Ephesians 3:20 NLT)

- For God knew his people in advance, and he chose them to become like his Son so that his Son would be firstborn [supreme] among many brothers and sisters. (Romans 8:29 NLT)

- Remain in me, and I will remain in you. For a branch cannot produce fruit if it is severed from the vine, and you cannot be fruitful unless you remain in me. (John 15:4 NLT)

Abiding
- Be still and know that I am God. (Psalm 46:10 NIV)

- Always be joyful. Never stop praying. Be thankful in all circumstances, for this is God's will for you who belong to Christ Jesus. (1 Thessalonians 5:16-18 NLT)

- Jesus said to the people who believed in him, "You are truly my disciples if you remain faithful to my teachings. And you will know the truth, and the truth will set you free." (John 8:31, 32 NLT)

Scripture References

Chapter 3 - Emergence

Into the Light

- Continue to work out your salvation with fear and trembling for it is God who works in you to will and to act according to his good purpose. (Philippians 2:12, 13 NIV)

- For we know how dearly God loves us, because he has given us the Holy Spirit to fill our hearts with his love. (Romans 5:5b NLT)

- Then Jesus said, "Come to me, all of you who are weary and carry heavy burdens, and I will give you rest. Take my yoke upon you. Let me teach you, because I am humble and gentle at heart, and you will find rest for your souls. For my yoke is easy to bear, and the burden I give you is light." (Matthew 11:28-30 NLT)

Freedom

- Jesus said to the people who believed in him, "You are truly my disciples if you remain faithful to my teachings. And you will know the truth, and the truth will set you free." (John 8:31, 32 NLT)

- In addition to all of these [armor of God], hold up the shield of faith to stop the fiery arrows of the devil. (Ephesians 6:16 NLT)

- So then, just as you received Christ Jesus as Lord, continue to live in him, rooted and built up in him, strengthened in the faith as you were taught, and overflowing with thankfulness. (Colossians 2:6, 7 NIV)

- Three different times I begged the Lord to take it away. Each time he said, "My grace is all you need. My power works in weakness." (2 Corinthians 12:8, 9 NLT)

- And so, dear brothers and sisters, I plead with you to give your bodies to God because of all he has done for you. Let them be a living and holy sacrifice. This is truly the way to worship him. (Romans 12:1 NLT)

- And then I heard the Lord asking, "Whom shall I send as a messenger to this people? Who will go for us?" And I said, "Here I am. Send me." (Isaiah 6:8 NLT)

- Can we boast, then, that we have done anything to be accepted by God? No, because our acquittal is not based on obeying the law. It is based on faith. (Romans 3:27 NLT)

- We know how much God loves us, and we have put our trust in his love. God is love, and all who live in love live in God, and God lives in them. And as we live in God, our love grows more perfect. So we will not be afraid on the day of judgement, but we can face him with confidence because we live like Jesus here in this world. Such love has no fear, because perfect love expels all fear. If we are afraid it is for fear of punishment, and this shows that we have not fully experienced his perfect love. (1 John 4:16-18)

Rest

- Then Jesus said, "Come to me, all of you who are weary and carry heavy burdens, and I will give you rest." (Matthew 11:28 NLT)

- Jesus sat down near the collection box in the Temple and watched as the crowds dropped in their money. Many rich people put in large amounts. Then a poor widow came and dropped in two small coins.

   Jesus called his disciples to him and said, "I tell you the truth, this poor widow has given more than all the others who are making contributions. For they gave a tiny part of their surplus, but she, poor as she is, has given everything she had to live on." (Mark 12:41-44 NLT)

- And if you give even a cup of cold water to one of the least of my followers, you will surely be rewarded. (Matthew 10:42 NLT)

- And the Holy Spirit helps us in our weakness. For example, we don't know what God wants us to pray for. But the holy Spirit prays for us with groaning that cannot be expressed in words. (Romans 8:26 NLT)

Chapter 4 - Final Word

Love

- If I could speak all the languages of earth and of angels, but didn't love others, I would only be a noisy gong or a clanging cymbal. If I had the gift of prophecy, and if I understood all of God's secret plans and possessed all knowledge, and if I had such faith that I could move mountains, but didn't love others, I would be nothing, If I gave everything I have to the poor and even sacrificed my body, I could boast about it; but if I didn't love others, I would have gained nothing. (1 Corinthians 13:1-3 NLT)

- People judge by outward appearance, but the Lord looks at the heart. (Samuel 16:7b NLT)

- Jesus called his disciples to him and said, "I tell you the truth, this poor widow has given more than all the others who are making contributions. For they gave a tiny part of their surplus, but she, poor as she is, has given everything she has to live on." (Mark 12:43, 44 NLT)

- God is love. When we take up permanent residence in a life of love, we live in God and God lives in us. This way, love has the run of the house, becomes at home and mature in us so that we're free of worry on Judgement Day— our standing in the world is identical with

Christ's. There is no room in love for fear. Well-formed love banishes fear. Since fear is crippling, a fearful life—fear of death, fear of judgment—is one not fully formed in love. (1 John 4:16-18 The Message)

- The only thing that counts is faith expressing itself through love. (Galatians 5:6 NIV)

Postscript

- I tell you the truth, anyone who sneaks over the wall of a sheepfold, rather than going through the gate, must surely be a thief and a robber! But the one who enters through the gate is the shepherd of the sheep. The gatekeeper opens the gate for him, and the sheep recognize his voice and come to him. He calls his own sheep by name and leads them out. After he has gathered his own flock he walks ahead of them, and they follow him because they know his voice. They won't follow a stranger; they will run from him because they don't know his voice. (John 10:2-5 NLT)

- And you will know the truth, and the truth will set you free. (John 8:32 NLT)

Appendix

Abraham

- Then the Lord said to him, "No, your servant will not be your heir, for you will have a son of your own who will be your heir." Then the Lord took Abram outside and said to him, "Look up into the sky and count the stars if you can. That's how many descendants you will have." (Genesis 15:4, 5 NLT)

- And Abram believed the Lord, and the Lord counted him as righteous because of his faith. (Genesis 15:6 NLT)

- But God replied, "No—Sarah, your wife, will give birth to a son for you. You will name him Isaac, and I will confirm my covenant with him and his descendants as an everlasting covenant." (Genesis 17:19 NLT)

- Abraham reasoned that if Isaac died, God was able to bring him back to life again, and in a sense, Abraham did receive his son back from the dead. (Hebrews 11:19 NLT)

- "Stay here with the donkey," Abraham told the servants. "The boy and I will travel a little farther. We will worship there, and then we will come right back." (Genesis 22:5 NLT)

- Abraham never wavered in believing God's promise. In fact, his faith grew stronger, and in this he brought glory to God. He was fully convinced that God is able to do whatever he promises. (Romans 4:20, 21 NLT)

- "Don't lay a hand on the boy!" the angel said. "Do not hurt him in any way, for now I know that you truly fear God. You have not withheld from me even your son, your only son." (Genesis 22:12)

- "You hypocrites! Isaiah was right when he prophesied about you, for he wrote, 'These people honor me with their lips, but their hearts are far from me. Their worship is a farce, for they teach man-made ideas as commands from God.'" (Matthew 15:7, 8; see also Isaiah 29:13)

- Romans 4: Read the entire chapter.

Achievement and Self-worth (no scripture references)

Christ, My Righteousness
- But now you must be holy in everything you do, just as God who chose you is holy. For the Scriptures say, "You must be holy because I am holy." (1 Peter 1:16 NLT)

- But the Holy Spirit produces this kind of fruit in our lives: love, joy, peace, patience, kindness, goodness, faithfulness, gentleness and self-control. (Galatians 5:22, 23a NLT)

- 1 Corinthians 13: full chapter

- God made him who had no sin to be sin for us, so that in him we might become the righteousness of God. (2 Corinthians 5:21 NIV)

- And because you belong to him, the power of the life-giving Spirit has freed you from the power of sin that leads to death. (Romans 8:2 NLT)

- My old self has been crucified with Christ. It is no longer I who live, but Christ lives in me. So I live in this earthly body by trusting in the Son of God, who loved me and gave himself for me. (Galatians 2:20 NLT)

- Therefore, my dear friends, as you have always obeyed—not only in my presence, but now much more in my absence—continue to work out your salvation with fear and trembling, for it is God who works in you to will and to act according to his good purpose. (Philippians 2:12, 13 NIV)

- So just as you received Christ Jesus as Lord, continue to live in him, rooted and built up in him, strengthened in the faith as you were taught, and overflowing with thankfulness. (Colossians 2:6 NIV)

Conviction and Condemnation
- Investigate my life, O God, find out everything about me; cross-examine and test me, get a clear picture of what I'm about; See for

Scripture References

yourself whether I've done anything wrong—and guide me on the road to eternal life. (Psalm 139:23, 24 The Message)

- But the one who enters through the gate is the shepherd of the sheep. The gatekeeper opens the gate for him, and the sheep recognize his voice and come to him. He calls his own sheep by name and leads them out. After he has gathered his own flock, he walks ahead of them, and they follow him because they know his voice. They won't follow a stranger; they will run from him because they don't know his voice. (John 10:2-5 NLT)

- For the accuser of our brothers and sisters has been thrown down to earth—the one who accuses them before our God day and night. (Revelation 12:10 NLT)

- So there is no condemnation for those who belong to Christ Jesus. (Romans 8:1 NLT)

- God saved you by his grace when you believed. And you can't take credit for this; it is a gift from God. (Ephesians 2:8 NLT)

- But if we are living in the light, as God is in the light, then we have fellowship with each other, and the blood of Jesus his Son, cleanses us from all sin. (1 John 1:7 NLT)

- Don't think you are better than you really are. Be honest in your evaluation of yourselves, measuring yourselves by the faith God has given us. (Romans 12:3 NLT)

Romans 8:28

- And we know that God causes everything to work together for the good of those who love God and are called according to his purpose for them. (Romans 8:28 NLT)

- I have told you all this so that you may have peace in me. Here on earth you will have many trials and sorrows. But take heart, because I have overcome the world. (John 16:33 NLT)

- You prepare a feast for me in the presence of my enemies. You honor me by anointing my head with oil. My cup overflows with blessings. (Psalm 23:5 NLT)

Wisdom

- Send out your light and your truth; let them guide me. Let them lead me to your holy mountain, to the place where you live. (Psalm 43:3 NLT)

- If you need wisdom, ask our generous God, and he will give it to you. He will not rebuke you for asking. (James 1:5 NLT)

- But the wisdom from above is first of all pure. It is also peace loving, gentle at all times, and willing to yield to others. It is full of mercy and good deeds. (James 3:17 NLT)

- Who can know the Lord's thoughts? Who knows enough to teach him? (1 Corinthians 2:16 NLT. See also Isaiah 40:13)

- Don't think you are better than you really are. Be honest in your evaluation of yourselves, measuring yourselves by the faith God has given us. (Romans 12:3 NLT)

- My child, listen to what I say, and treasure my commands. Tune your ears to wisdom and concentrate on understanding. Cry out for insight, and ask for understanding. Search for them as you would for silver; seek them like hidden treasures. Then you will understand what it means to fear the Lord, and you will gain knowledge of God. For the Lord grants wisdom! From his mouth come knowledge and understanding. (Proverbs 2:1-6 NLT)

- And we know that God causes everything to work together for the good of those who love God and are called according to his purpose for them. (Romans 8:28 NLT)

About the Author

J. Lauraine Johnson is a retired elementary school teacher and teacher of English Language Learners (ELL). She has had involvements with the organizations Young Life and Intervarsity Christian Fellowship. Janice is a life-long learner, whether it be reading, playing the piano, or developing a proficiency in French. She enjoys a walk in the woods, camping, and winter sports. An unexpected knock at the door is one of her favourite things, and a houseful of people gives her great pleasure. J. Lauraine Johnson lives with her husband, Gord, in British Columbia, Canada.

Contact: jlaurainejohnson@gmail.com

www.ingramcontent.com/pod-product-compliance
Lightning Source LLC
Chambersburg PA
CBHW071400080526
44587CB00017B/3150